TREETOPS CL

DR JEKYLL AND MR HYDE

ROBERT LOUIS STEVENSON

adapted by Alan MacDonald

OXFORD
UNIVERSITY PRESS

OXFORD
UNIVERSITY PRESS

Great Clarendon Street, Oxford OX2 6DP

Oxford University Press is a department of the University of Oxford.
It furthers the University's objective of excellence in research, scholarship,
and education by publishing worldwide in

Oxford New York
Auckland Cape Town Dar es Salaam Hong Kong Karachi
Kuala Lumpur Madrid Melbourne Mexico City Nairobi
New Delhi Shanghai Taipei Toronto

With offices in

Argentina Austria Brazil Chile Czech Republic France Greece
Guatemala Hungary Italy Japan Poland Portugal Singapore
South Korea Switzerland Thailand Turkey Ukraine Vietnam

Oxford is a registered trade mark of Oxford University Press
in the UK and in certain other countries

First published 2001
This edition published 2006

British Library Cataloguing in Publication Data
Data available

ISBN : 978-0-19-918491-0

5 7 9 10 8 6 4

Cover: Mark Edwards
Inside illustrations: Martin McKenna

Printed in Great Britain by Ashford Colour Press, Gosport, Hants

Paper used in the production of this book is a natural, recyclable product
made from wood grown in sustainable forests. The manufacturing process
conforms to the environmental regulations of the country of origin.

About the Author

ROBERT LOUIS STEVENSON
1850 – 1894

Robert Louis Stevenson was born in Edinburgh in 1850. From an early age he suffered from bad health. After leaving university he travelled abroad to escape from Scotland's cold and wet climate. His first books were about his travels in Belgium and France.

In his thirties Stevenson achieved fame with his adventure tale *Treasure Island.* The novel, published in 1883, about pirates and buried treasure, was an instant success. Three years later Stevenson followed it with *The Strange Case of Dr Jekyll and Mr Hyde.*

Stevenson said the idea for the book came to him in a dream. A friend describes him coming down to lunch one day in a preoccupied state of mind and hurrying his meal (something he rarely did). Stevenson announced that he had to return to work on a story that he was eager to complete. He was not to be interrupted even if the house was on fire!

The result was one of the most chilling horror stories ever written.

PROLOGUE

The Last Will and Testament of

DR HENRY JEKYLL

23rd May 1886

I, Henry Jekyll, declare that in the event of my death, all my possessions are to pass into the hands of my friend, Edward Hyde.

In the case of my disappearance or unexplained absence for a period of more than three months, I wish that Edward Hyde shall step into my shoes without further delay.

Henry Jekyll MD, DCL

CHAPTER I

The Story of the Door

Mr Utterson, the lawyer, was a man who never smiled and spent his words as rarely as gold. Tall, lean, and craggy faced, there was still something likeable about him. At a supper party, when he'd drunk a little wine, a spark of warmth entered his eye that was missing from his conversation.

Utterson liked order and good sense, which was why the will of his friend Henry Jekyll offended him. Jekyll had made him promise never to discuss the subject of his will. As a lawyer, Utterson had refused to have anything to do with the drawing up of the document. Yet there it lay at the back of his safe. When he thought of the will a shadow crossed his face. He recalled the mysterious references to Jekyll's possible 'disappearance' and the man called Hyde 'stepping into his shoes'. What could these things mean? Utterson had never met Edward Hyde and knew nothing about him. Nothing that is, until one Sunday he stumbled across the name by sheer chance.

◆◆◆

On most Sundays Utterson went walking with his friend and cousin, Richard Enfield. On this occasion their ramble took them into a back street of a busy quarter of London. The neighbourhood was run down, but the street looked prosperous with its freshly painted shutters and polished brass name-plates. Two doors from the corner of the street, one building cast a shadow over the brightness of the rest. It was two storeys high and had no windows – only a door with the paint peeling and stained. There was no bell or knocker on the door. Tramps often sheltered in its entrance and children played upon the steps without anyone to disturb them.

Utterson and Enfield paused in their walk outside the eyeless house.

'Did you ever notice that door?' asked Enfield. 'It's connected with a very odd story.'

A worried look crossed Utterson's face. 'Indeed?' he said. 'And what was that?'

'Well, it happened this way,' replied Enfield. 'I was coming home about three o'clock on a bleak winter morning. My way took me through a part of town where the streets seemed as empty as a church. Eventually I got into that state of mind where you listen and listen for every footstep and begin to long for the sight of a policeman. All at once I saw two figures. One was a little man stumping along at a brisk pace, the other was a young girl of eight or ten, running hard in the opposite direction. Well, naturally enough the two ran straight into each other at the corner.

'Was the girl hurt?' asked Utterson.

'That was the worst part,' replied Enfield. 'The man trampled right over her. I saw him stamp on her quite deliberately. He left her screaming on the ground while he went on his way, regardless.'

'Did you chase after him?' said Utterson.

'Certainly and caught him, too,' said Enfield. 'I

brought him back to where a group had already gathered around the crying child. They turned out to be the girl's family. Pretty soon, the doctor turned up, too. The girl had been sent to fetch him and was on her way back.'

'The doctor examined the child?' asked Utterson.

'Yes, she wasn't badly hurt,' said Enfield, 'more frightened than anything, but her attacker seemed perfectly cool about the whole business. I felt a deep loathing for him, from the very first moment. What's more I could see the same hatred in the eyes of the family and even the doctor. Every time he looked at my prisoner, I saw him turn sick and white as if he couldn't stand the sight of him. We told the man that we would make such a scandal about his behaviour that his name would be mud throughout London. And all the while we threatened and shouted, the man stood in the middle, staring us out with a kind of sneering coolness. He was scared all right, but he carried it off like the devil himself. "If you choose to make a scene out of this accident," he said, "I am helpless. No gentleman wishes to lose his good name. Name your price." Well we pushed him up to a hundred pounds for the girl's family. The next thing was to get the money. And where do you think he took us?'

'Where?' asked Utterson, although the look on his face suggested he knew the answer.

'To this very door we're standing outside,' said Enfield. 'He pulled out a key and went inside. A few minutes later he came back with ten pounds in gold and a cheque for the rest of the amount.'

'A large sum of money,' said Utterson, shaking his head.

'Exactly,' said Enfield. 'But the name on the cheque was a person who could well afford it. The name I can't mention – but it's a very well-known name.'

'And was the cheque genuine?' asked Utterson.

'My thought exactly,' said Enfield. 'I pointed out to the fellow that the whole business smelled of a trick. A man doesn't go into a door at four in the morning and come back with someone else's cheque for £90 as easy as winking. Yet, here's the odd thing, when we took the cheque to the bank, it was quite genuine.'

'Even worse!' said the lawyer.

'Indeed,' said Enfield. 'It's a bad story. Because the man I've described was a really vile, ugly character, and yet the man who signed the cheque is a highly respected person. Someone who does a lot of good, in fact. I can only guess that our friend must have been blackmailing him.'

'And you don't know if the person who signed the cheque lives there?' asked Utterson.

'He doesn't. I happened to notice his address was in

some square or other,' replied Enfield.

'And you have never asked him about the place with the door?'

'No, I make it a rule where bad business is involved never to ask questions.'

'A very good rule, too,' said Utterson with a note of relief.

'But I've kept an eye on this place,' Enfield went on. 'There is no other door, and no one goes in or out, except once in a while the villain I've told you about.'

They walked on for a while in silence. Utterson was evidently much affected by his friend's story. Eventually he said, 'Enfield, that's a good rule of yours about not asking questions. Nevertheless, I want to ask the name of the man that knocked down the girl.'

'I can't see the harm in that,' said Enfield. 'His name was Hyde.'

'Hmm,' said Utterson. 'And what does this Hyde look like?'

'He is hard to describe. There's something wrong about his appearance. Something that's ugly, displeasing. I never saw a man I disliked so much and yet I can't explain why. He's a strange-looking fellow I'll say that, though I can't quite put my finger on what's strange about him.'

The pair walked on again in silence, with Utterson

deep in thought.

'You're quite sure he had a key?' he asked finally.

'My dear sir . . . ' began Enfield.

'I'm sorry, I know my questions sound strange,' said Utterson. 'But there's a reason I haven't asked you for the name of the other man involved. It's because I already know it.'

'You might have warned me,' replied Enfield, a touch sulkily. 'But everything I've told you is true to the last detail. The man had a key and what's more I saw him use it only a week ago.'

Utterson sighed deeply but said nothing. Presently, it was Enfield who broke the silence again. 'Here's a lesson to me to hold my tongue in future. Let's make a bargain never to talk about this affair again.'

'I will shake hands on that with all my heart,' said the lawyer. 'And I'd be grateful, Enfield, if you would not pursue your curiosity in this matter any further. It's a matter of a friend's good name.'

'Of course,' said Enfield. 'Not another word about it.'

Soon after that the two men parted company. Utterson went back to his house with a heavy heart. He was thinking again of the strange will at the back of his safe: the will of Doctor Henry Jekyll.

CHAPTER 2

The Search for Mr Hyde

Utterson took out the long brown envelope from the back of his safe and studied the will again. There was the sinister name of Edward Hyde, linked to Henry Jekyll's. And there was the clause that worried him so much, stating that if Jekyll ever disappeared, Edward Hyde should 'step into his shoes without delay'. There could be no doubt that the man who signed the cheque in Enfield's story was Henry Jekyll. And that only deepened the worrying impression that Edward Hyde had some kind of hold over him. It was bad enough when Utterson knew nothing about Hyde, now he knew the man's ugly character the case only seemed worse.

'I thought it was madness,' muttered Utterson, 'but now I fear it is disgrace.'

With that he blew out his candle, put on his coat and set out for Cavendish Square where his friend, the great Doctor Lanyon lived. Like Utterson, Lanyon had known Henry Jekyll since college days. 'If anyone knows, it will be Lanyon,' the lawyer thought to himself.

Utterson found Dr Lanyon sitting alone over a bottle of wine. Lanyon was a red-faced man, with a shock of white hair and a bold, decisive manner. Seeing Utterson, he jumped up from his chair and shook hands warmly. The two were old friends and were fond of each other's company.

After a little rambling talk, the lawyer led up to the subject on his mind.

'I suppose, Lanyon, you and I must be the two oldest friends that Henry Jekyll has.'

'No need to mention the old,' laughed Lanyon, 'but I suppose we are. What of it? I hardly see him nowadays.'

'Indeed?' said Utterson. 'I thought you and Jekyll shared a common interest in science.'

'We did,' Lanyon replied.' But it's more than ten years since Jekyll became too fanciful for my liking. He started to go wrong, very wrong. I've seen very little of the man of late. Such unscientific balderdash!' added the doctor, suddenly flushing purple with anger.

Utterson was taken aback by this outburst. What could Jekyll have done that was so deeply offensive to Lanyon? Surely it cannot be that bad, he thought to himself. They've probably only fallen out on some point of science. After a few seconds he put the question he'd come to ask.

'Did you ever come across a friend of his – one Edward Hyde?' he asked.

'Hyde?' repeated Lanyon. 'No, never heard of him. Not in my life.'

That was the only information the lawyer came away with. That night he slept badly, tossing and turning in his bed. When he did sleep, he dreamt of Edward Hyde. He saw the small dark figure walking swiftly through the city. Then the child running. Then Hyde trampling the child underfoot and passing on, deaf to the child's cries. Or else, he saw his friend Jekyll asleep in a wealthy house, the door of his bedroom opened, the curtains of the bed were pulled back and there was Hyde standing over him. And in all these nightmares, the figure of Hyde had no face.

From that night on, Utterson was seized with an overwhelming desire to meet Hyde face to face. If he could just set eyes on the real Mr Hyde then he felt the mystery would start to unravel. Early in the morning, at noon, and at night under the foggy moon, Utterson began to haunt the street of the door, hoping to glimpse his prey. 'If he be Mr Hyde,' he thought, 'I shall be Mr Seek.'

◆◆◆

Finally, one night the lawyer's patience was rewarded. It was a chill, frosty night. By ten o'clock when Utterson was at his post, the shops were closed and the streets were empty. The lawyer's attention was suddenly caught by an odd, light footstep drawing nearer. The steps grew louder as they turned the corner and came into the court.

At last Utterson could see a figure approaching the doorway. He was small and plainly dressed. Even at a distance, there was something about him that made the lawyer shudder. As he crossed the road, the man drew a key from his pocket to unlock the door. Utterson stepped out from his hiding place in the shadows and tapped him on the shoulder.

'Mr Hyde, I think?'

Hyde shrank back with a hissing gasp of breath.

He avoided looking up but he answered coolly enough.

'That is my name. What do you want?'

'I am an old friend of Dr Jekyll's, Mr Utterson of Gaunt Street. You must have heard my name. I thought you might ask me in.'

'You won't find Dr Jekyll, he's not at home,' replied Mr Hyde, putting his key in the lock. Then suddenly he added, 'How did you know me?'

'I'll answer that,' said Utterson, 'but in return will you show me your face?'

Mr Hyde hesitated, then turned around suddenly with an air of bold defiance. For a few seconds the two men stared at each other.

'Now I shall know you again,' said Utterson. 'It may be useful.'

'Yes,' replied Hyde. 'It's as well we have met. You should have my address.' He gave the name of a street in Soho.

'Good heavens!' thought Utterson with a shudder, 'Is he thinking about the will?' But he kept his thoughts to himself and only grunted in reply to the address.

'And now,' said Hyde, 'your answer – how did you know me?'

'By description,' said Utterson.

'Whose description?'

'We have common friends.'

'Common friends?' scoffed Hyde. 'Who are they?'

'Jekyll for instance,' said the lawyer.

'He never told you!' cried Hyde angrily. 'I didn't think you'd have lied!'

'Come, that is no way to talk,' replied Utterson.

Hyde gave a savage laugh and the next moment had darted into the house and locked the door.

The lawyer stood for a while in the street, thinking, then he began to make his way home. Every now and again he put his hand to his head like a man trying to solve a baffling puzzle. The problem bothering him was this: why had he felt such loathing and disgust when talking to Hyde? It was true that Hyde was pale and undersized, he had a displeasing smile and behaved with an odd mixture of fear and boldness. It was true that he spoke with a husky, broken voice. Yet none of these points explained why Utterson should feel so revolted by him.

There must be something else, thought the lawyer. The man seems hardly human! But oh my poor, Jekyll! If ever I saw the devil's mark on a face, it's on that of your new friend.

Round the corner from the back street, there was a square of ancient handsome houses. In fact the door Hyde had entered led by a back way into one of these.

Mr Utterson now stopped at the door of this wealthy-looking house and knocked. A servant opened the door.

'Is Dr Jekyll at home, Poole?' asked the lawyer.

'I will see, Mr Utterson,' said Poole. Utterson was left in a hall with a warm, crackling fire while the servant

went away. Soon after, Poole returned to say Dr Jekyll had gone out.

'I saw Mr Hyde go in by the old door to the laboratory. Is that right, when Dr Jekyll is not at home?'

'Quite right,' said Poole. 'Mr Hyde has a key.'

'Your master seems to put a lot of trust in him,' said Utterson.

'Yes sir, he do indeed. We all have orders to obey him,' said Poole.

Utterson nodded. He was curious to know Poole's impression of the mysterious Hyde, so he made no mention of where he'd just come from.

'I do not think I ever met this Mr Hyde,' he said.

'Oh dear no, sir. He's not the kind of gentleman my master would invite to dinner. We see little of him on this side of the house. He mostly comes and goes by the laboratory.'

'Thank you. Well goodnight, Poole.'

'Goodnight, Mr Utterson.'

The lawyer set off home with a heavy heart. The more he knew of Hyde the less he liked the whole sinister business.

Poor Henry Jekyll, he thought. He was wild when he was young. Perhaps it's the ghost of some old crime that gives Hyde such a hold on him. Yet Hyde must have secrets of his own, dark secrets by the look of him. It makes my blood run cold to think of Enfield's story. That creature stealing like a thief to Henry's bedside in the dead of the night, demanding money. And the danger of it! If Hyde suspects about the will, he might get impatient for Jekyll to die. I must find a way to help my friend, if only he'll let me. Once more his thoughts were drawn back to Henry Jekyll's will and the strange, disturbing terms that were set down there.

CHAPTER 3

A Private Talk with Dr Jekyll

Two weeks later, by a stroke of good luck, Dr Jekyll gave a dinner party for a few friends. Mr Utterson was one of the party and stayed behind afterwards for a word in private with Jekyll.

The two old friends sat by the fire after the other guests had gone home. Dr Jekyll was a large, smooth-faced man of about fifty. There was cleverness and kindness in his face and it was obvious that he was genuinely fond of Utterson.

'I have been wanting to speak to you, Jekyll,' began Utterson. 'It's about that will of yours.'

The subject was obviously one that the doctor disliked, but he answered lightly, 'My poor Utterson, I never saw a man so upset as you were by my will, unless it was Lanyon with what he called my scientific heresies. Oh you needn't frown! I know Lanyon's a good fellow, but an ignorant, narrow-minded one for all that. I've never been so disappointed in a man as Lanyon.'

Utterson ignored this and stuck rigidly to his subject. 'You know I never approved of it?'

'My will?' said the doctor, rather sharply. 'Of course, you told me so at the time.'

'Well, I'll tell you again,' said Utterson. 'I've been learning something about your Mr Hyde.'

At this, the wide handsome face of Jekyll turned pale. Even his lips were ashen.

'I don't wish to hear any more,' he said. 'This is a subject we agreed to drop.'

'What I heard about Hyde was appalling,' continued Utterson, doggedly.

'It makes no difference. You don't understand my situation,' replied the doctor. 'My position is a very strange and painful one, Utterson. It's one that can't be improved by talking.'

'Jekyll,' said Utterson warmly. 'You know me. I'm a man who can be trusted. Tell me in confidence what trouble you're in. I'm willing to stake my life that I can get you out of it.'

'My dear Utterson, that is very good of you,' said the doctor. 'Believe me, I would trust you more than any man in the world. But the matter isn't what you imagine. And just to put your mind at rest, I will tell you one thing. I can be rid of Hyde any time I choose, I give you my word on that. Now, don't be offended but this is a private matter and I'd rather you left it alone.'

Utterson stared gloomily into the fire for a while. 'I've

no doubt you're perfectly right,' he said at last and got to his feet.

'Well, since you've raised this subject,' said Jekyll, 'there's one last thing I'd like to ask. I have a very great interest in poor Hyde. I know you've met him because he told me so. And I know he was rude to you. But I do take a real interest in that young man, and if I'm ever taken away, I'd like you to see that he gets his rights. It would be a great weight off my mind if you'd promise that.'

Utterson frowned. 'I can't pretend I shall ever like him,' he said.

'I don't ask that,' said the doctor, laying his hand on Utterson's arm. 'I only ask you to help him, for my sake.'

Utterson heaved a sigh. 'Very well, I promise,' he said.

CHAPTER 4

The Carew Murder Case

It was almost a year after Utterson's talk with Jekyll that London was shocked by a vicious crime. The murder caused a great scandal because the victim was a well-known MP.

The details of the crime were supplied by a maid who had witnessed it. She lived in a house not far from the River Thames. Some time after eleven o'clock she'd been sitting at her window, looking out dreamily on a full moon. The night was clear and cloudless and she'd never felt more at peace with the world. As she sat there, she saw an old white-haired gentleman coming along the lane, and a very small man approaching from the opposite direction. When they got within speaking distance they met just under the maid's eyes. The old man bowed and made some remark in a polite manner. From the way he was pointing he may have been asking the way. The full moon shone on his face and the girl felt there was something kind and gracious about him. At last her eye wandered to the smaller man and she was surprised to recognize him as a certain Mr Hyde. He had once visited her master and she'd taken an instant dislike to him. Hyde was listening to the gentleman with obvious impatience. He never answered a word, but played all the time with a heavy cane in his hand.

All of a sudden, Hyde seemed to break out in a wild temper. He stamped his foot and brandished his cane, spitting out words like a wild animal. Astonished, the old gentleman took a step back. That was when Hyde lost all control and clubbed him to the ground. The maid remembered seeing a storm of blows rain down on the victim before she fainted away at the sheer horror of the sight.

It was two o'clock in the morning before she came to herself and called for the police. The murderer had fled the scene but his victim still lay lifeless in the road. The wooden cane that had been used as a weapon had broken clean in two. One half had rolled into the gutter, the other half had vanished with the murderer. The

police searched the victim and found a purse and a gold watch – robbery evidently wasn't in the killer's mind. There was also a sealed and stamped envelope in his pocket that bore the name and address of Mr Utterson.

The police brought the envelope to the lawyer early the next morning. Utterson dressed quickly and heard their story with deepening anxiety. 'And the victim?' he asked. 'You don't know his identity?' The police officer shook his head. 'We were hoping you could help us with that, sir.'

Utterson nodded. He was shocked and worried by the whole tale. If Hyde had really committed this horrible crime, then it meant that Henry Jekyll was linked to a murderer. Until he knew the truth, Utterson felt he should be careful what he told the police.

'I can say nothing until I have seen the body,' he said. 'This may be very serious.'

At the police station Utterson took one look at the dead man's bruised face and turned away, covering his mouth with a handkerchief.

'Are you all right, sir?' asked the officer.

'Yes, yes, I recognize him,' said Utterson. 'I am sorry to say that this is Sir Danvers Carew.'

'Good God, sir!' exclaimed the police officer. 'The MP? This will be all over the papers. And perhaps, sir, you can lead us to the murderer,' he added with a gleam of ambition.

Utterson had been worried by the first mention of Hyde's name in the tale. Now seeing the broken wooden cane, he was certain that Jekyll was involved – even if only by connection to a murderer. The cane was a present Utterson himself had given to Henry Jekyll many years before. The lawyer said nothing of this to the police.

'If you'll come with me, I think I can lead you to

Hyde's house,' he told the officer.

By this time it was nine o'clock in the morning and a great brown fog hung over London. The quarter of Soho where Hyde lived seemed to Utterson like some outer region of hell. The swirling, muddy fog held the city in its clammy fingers.

Hyde's address was in a dingy street lined by shabby shops and cheap cafés. Ragged children huddled in the doorways for warmth. This was the home of Henry

Jekyll's favourite – the heir to a quarter of a million pounds.

The door was opened by a silvery-haired old woman. Her face was hard and sly but her manners were well polished. 'Yes, Mr Hyde lives here, but he's not at home,' she told them. She said Hyde had come in late that night and gone away again in less than an hour. His habits were very irregular and he was often absent for weeks or months at a time.

'Very well then, we'd like to see his rooms,' said the lawyer. 'This is Inspector Newcomen of Scotland Yard.'

The old woman's face lit up with cruel pleasure. 'Ah! He is in trouble! What has he done?'

'He don't seem very popular, does he?' the inspector remarked to Utterson. He turned back to the housekeeper. 'Now stand aside, my good woman, and let us see the rooms.'

Mr Hyde had only used two rooms in the whole house but these were richly furnished. There was fine wine in a cabinet, paintings on the walls, and the carpets were thick and costly. However, the rooms looked as if they'd been turned upside down by someone in a great hurry. Clothes were strewn about the floor and drawers lay open. In the fire a pile of grey ashes suggested someone had recently burnt a pile of papers. The inspector picked out the butt of a green chequebook from the embers.

When they searched the room, they found the other half of the broken cane behind the door. Inspector Newcomen was delighted. His satisfaction was complete when they visited the bank and found several thousand pounds in Hyde's account.

'I have him in my sights, you can count on it, sir,' he told Utterson. 'He must have lost his head, leaving that cane behind. As for the chequebook, that was his worst mistake. We have only to keep watch at the bank and he'll turn up sooner or later to draw out his money.'

Yet despite the policeman's confidence, catching Hyde proved to be far from simple.

It seemed that the murderer had no friends and no family that could be traced. He had never been photographed and few people had more than a passing acquaintance with him. The only point that every witness agreed upon was that Hyde made a bad impression on them.

CHAPTER 5

A Letter from Hyde

Later that same day Mr Utterson paid a visit to Dr Jekyll's house. Poole, the butler, let him in and led him across the back yard to the building known as the laboratory. It was the first time the lawyer had seen this part of his friend's domain and he gazed round curiously. The building was dingy and windowless. It had once been a surgeon's operating room crowded with eager students. Now it was cold and silent, the tables cluttered with Jekyll's chemical apparatus.

Poole took Utterson up some stairs at the far end to a door that led to the doctor's office. It was a large room lit by three dusty windows barred with iron. These looked out on the court below. Dr Jekyll himself sat by the fire looking deathly pale. He did not rise to welcome his visitor but only held out a cold hand.

'You've heard the news?' asked Utterson as soon as Poole had gone.

The doctor shuddered. 'The newsboys were crying it in the square. I heard them from my dining room.'

'One question,' said Utterson. 'Sir Danvers Carew was my client, but so are you, and I need to know what I'm doing. Tell me you haven't been mad enough to hide this murderer.'

'Utterson I swear to God I am finished with Hyde,' cried the doctor. 'On my honour I will have nothing more to do with him. Indeed he doesn't want my help. You don't know him like I do, he's safe, quite safe. You'll never hear of him again.'

'You seem pretty sure of him,' said Utterson. 'I hope you're right. If it comes to a trial your name might be mentioned.'

'I'm quite sure of him,' said Jekyll. 'Though I can't tell you my reasons. There is, however, one thing I'd like your advice on. I've received a letter and I'm not sure whether to show it to the police. I want to put it in your hands, Utterson. I trust you completely.'

'You're afraid it will lead to Hyde's arrest?' asked the lawyer.

'After what has happened I can't say I care what happens to Hyde,' replied Jekyll. 'I was thinking more about myself.'

'Let me see the letter,' said Utterson.

The letter was written in odd, upright handwriting.

Utterson felt some relief reading this letter. It placed Jekyll's relationship with Hyde in a better light than he had expected. He even blamed himself for some of his past suspicions.

Dear Dr Jekyll

I cannot thank you enough for your thousand generosities to me which have been repaid so unworthily. You need have no concern for my safety since I have means of escape in which I place all my trust.

Your humble servant

Edward Hyde

'Have you kept the envelope?' he asked.

'No, I burned it without thinking,' replied Jekyll. 'But there was no postmark, it was delivered by hand.'

'Shall I keep this letter and think it over?' asked Utterson.

'Whatever you decide. I've lost all faith in my own judgement,' said Jekyll.

'One last question,' said Utterson. 'Was it Hyde who dictated that part in your will about your disappearance?'

The colour drained from the doctor's face and he nodded dumbly.

'I knew it,' said Utterson. 'He was planning to murder you. You have had a narrow escape.'

'I've had more than that,' said the doctor solemnly. 'I've had a lesson. Oh God, Utterson, what a lesson I have had!' And he covered his face in his hands.

◆◆◆

On his way out Utterson stopped for a word with Poole.

'By the way,' he said, 'there was a letter delivered by hand today. What was the messenger like?' Poole was certain that nothing had come that day except a few bills by post. This news sent the lawyer home still feeling uneasy. Plainly the letter must have been delivered to the laboratory door. Perhaps it had even been written in the doctor's office. As he made his way home, the newsboys were crying, 'Special Edition. Shocking murder of an MP!'

Utterson turned his mind to the awkward decision he had to make. Should he hand the letter over to the police? Would it help Jekyll or simply drag him into the murder investigation? For once in his life he felt in need of another person's advice.

Later that evening he sat with Mr Guest, his head clerk. Outside the brown fog still lapped around the city but inside the room was lit by a cheering fire. Utterson had opened a bottle of a very good wine that they were drinking. There was no man the lawyer trusted more than his clerk. Since Guest was a great expert on handwriting, it seemed a natural step to ask his opinion.

'This is a sad business about Sir Danvers,' began Utterson.

'Yes, sir, indeed,' replied Guest. 'The murderer was obviously a madman.'

'I should like your opinion on that,' replied Utterson. 'I happen to have a letter here in his handwriting. This is between ourselves, of course, because I'm not sure what to do with it. But there it is, a murderer's signature, right in your line I should say.'

Guest's eyes brightened with curiosity and he took the letter and examined it eagerly.

'No, sir,' he said, 'not mad, but it is odd handwriting.'

'And by all accounts a very odd writer,' remarked Utterson.

Just then the servant entered with a note.

'Is that from Dr Jekyll?' asked the clerk. 'I thought I recognized the handwriting. Is it a private matter?'

'Only an invitation to dinner,' replied Utterson. 'Why, do you want to see it?'

'Thank you, sir.' Guest took Jekyll's note and laid it alongside the letter from Hyde. For a minute he studied the two pieces of paper closely. At last he returned them both to his master. 'Thank you, sir. Very interesting,' he said.

'Why did you want to compare them?' asked Utterson.

'Well, sir, there's a rather unusual similarity. In fact the two pieces of handwriting are almost identical, except that they slope in a different way.'

'Rather odd,' said Utterson.

'As you say, sir, rather odd,' replied Guest.

'I wouldn't speak of this letter to anyone, you know,' said the lawyer, nervously.

'No, sir, I quite understand,' said the clerk.

As soon as Guest had gone, Mr Utterson took the letter and locked it away in his safe. What? he thought. Henry Jekyll forge a letter for a murderer? His blood ran cold in his veins.

CHAPTER 6

The Strange Incident of Dr Lanyon

It seemed that Mr Hyde had vanished as if he'd never existed. Despite thousands of pounds offered in reward money, the search for the murderer drew a blank. Much of Hyde's past came to light – and all the tales were of cruelty and violence – but there was no whisper of where he could be. From the morning he'd left the house in Soho after the murder, it was as if Hyde had melted into thin air.

◆◆◆

As the weeks wore on Mr Utterson began to recover his peace of mind. Now that Hyde's evil influence was gone, Dr Jekyll returned to his old life. He went out more, invited friends round for dinner, and generally seemed at ease. He devoted more of his time to helping others less fortunate and gave his money generously. This period of calm went on for two months. On the 8th January Utterson was at a dinner party at the doctor's house. Lanyon was also there and the three of them behaved like old friends again. Yet four days later Utterson was amazed to find Jekyll's door shut against him. For the next week the lawyer called daily at Jekyll's house but was turned away each time. Utterson had got used to seeing his friend every day and couldn't understand this abrupt change. He feared that Hyde might be the cause but no one had seen that evil figure since the murder.

Finally, Utterson paid a visit to Dr Lanyon. There a second rude shock was in store for him. In the space of a week Lanyon had changed from a healthy man to one who looked at death's door. His rosy face had grown pale and he was visibly balder and older. Worse than this, something in his behaviour suggested he was in the grip of some terrible fear. Utterson was deeply disturbed by his friend's rapid decline.

When he remarked that Lanyon didn't look well, the doctor declared he was a doomed man.

'I have had a great shock and I shall never recover,' he said. 'It's only a question of weeks.'

Utterson hardly knew how to respond to such an announcement.

'But surely . . . ' he mumbled. 'Surely . . . something can be done?'

'Thank you, but you forget I'm a doctor,' replied Lanyon with a dry laugh. 'Well, life has been good to me, I used to enjoy it. Yet I sometimes think if we knew the whole truth, we should be more eager to die.'

'Jekyll is ill, too,' said Utterson. 'Have you seen him?'

Lanyon's face set in a grim mask and he held up a trembling hand. 'I don't wish to see or hear any more of Dr Jekyll. I'm done with him, and I beg you not to mention someone I regard as dead.'

Once again Utterson was taken aback. After a long pause he asked, 'Can't I do anything? We three are such old friends, Lanyon, we won't live to make others.'

'Nothing can be done,' replied Lanyon. 'Ask Jekyll.'

'He won't see me,' said the lawyer.

'I'm not surprised,' said Lanyon. 'Some day, Utterson, after I'm dead, you may learn the truth of all this. I cannot tell you now. Meanwhile if you can stay and talk about anything else, for pity's sake do. But if you want to talk about Jekyll, I beg you to leave now, for I cannot bear it.'

As soon as he got home Utterson sat down and wrote to Jekyll. He complained that he never saw him and asked how he had fallen out with Dr Lanyon.

An answering letter came the next day. It was full of dark, mysterious hints that were not fully explained. Jekyll said that the quarrel with Lanyon could not be mended.

I do not blame our old friend, but I agree that Lanyon and I must never meet again.

From now on I must lead the life of a hermit. You mustn't be surprised, my dear friend, if my door is shut even to you. I have brought on myself a punishment and a danger that I cannot name. Pity me in my suffering. I never believed that earth could contain such terrors as I have known. The one thing you can do to help me, Utterson, is to leave me alone.

Utterson was amazed. A week ago the doctor had behaved as if nothing could be wrong in the world, now suddenly he had changed. His peace of mind was gone and his life was a sad wreck. Utterson wondered if Jekyll had gone mad. Yet in view of what Lanyon had said, he believed there must be some deeper cause.

Within a fortnight Dr Lanyon had taken to his bed and died. The night after the funeral Utterson retired to his office, in a low state of mind. He locked the door and drew out an envelope addressed to him in Lanyon's handwriting.

'*PRIVATE: for the eyes of J G Utterson ALONE* and in the *case of his death to be destroyed unread,*' said the writing. Utterson dreaded to read what was inside. 'I have buried one friend today,' he thought, 'what's inside this letter may cost me another.' Setting aside such fears, he opened the envelope. Inside was a second envelope sealed like the first. This one said, '*Not to be opened until the death or disappearance of Dr Henry Jekyll.*' Utterson stared at it. There was that word again: 'disappearance', the same word that appeared in the mad will of Jekyll's which Utterson had long ago returned to its owner. What did it mean? Utterson was seized with a strong desire to ignore the words on the envelope, tear it open, and read the secrets inside. Yet professional honour and duty to his dead friend stopped him. He put the packet back in the corner of his safe.

After that night Utterson was less eager to visit Jekyll's house. Part of him dreaded to know what was happening in that silent house of imprisonment. Poole often spoke to him on the doorstep but he had no good news to offer. Dr Jekyll more than ever kept to his office over the laboratory where he sometimes even slept. He was low in spirits and seemed to have some great weight on his mind. Little by little Utterson's visits began to tail off.

CHAPTER 7

The Face at the Window

Not long after, Utterson and Enfield were out on one of their regular Sunday walks. By chance they passed through the back street where Enfield had first told Utterson the story of Hyde. They stopped at the door to gaze at it.

'Well,' said Enfield, 'thankfully that story's over. We shall never see Mr Hyde again.'

'I hope not,' said Utterson. 'Did I ever tell you that I once met him and felt exactly the same loathing that you described?'

'It was impossible to feel anything else,' said Enfield. 'And, by the way, what a fool you must have thought me. I had no idea that this door was a back way into Jekyll's.'

'So you found that out, did you?' said Utterson. 'Then why don't we step into the court together and take a look at the windows of Jekyll's house. To tell the truth I've been worried about him.'

Utterson spoke all this with a casual air, yet inside he was feeling far from calm. Just standing outside the door reawoke stirrings of fear and dread within him. At that moment he was more grateful for Enfield's company than he'd ever been in his life. Yet he could not explain to his friend the full facts behind his concern for Jekyll.

The court was cool and damp in the evening twilight. The middle of one of the three windows was half way open and there sitting beside it, was the figure of a man taking the air like the loneliest of prisoners.

'Jekyll!' cried Utterson. 'I hope you are feeling better.'

'I am very low, Utterson,' said Jekyll in a weary voice. 'Very low. It will not last long thank God.'

'You stay indoors too much,' said the lawyer. 'You should be out getting some fresh air like Mr Enfield and myself. Why don't you get your hat and take a brisk walk with us?'

'You are very kind,' said Jekyll. 'I should very much like to, but no, no, it's impossible. I dare not. But I am really very glad to see you, Utterson. This is a great pleasure. I would ask you to come up but the place is not fit for visitors.'

'Why then,' said the lawyer, 'we shall stay down here and speak to you through the window.'

'Just what I was about to suggest . . . ' said the doctor with a weak smile. Yet the words were hardly out of his

mouth when his expression changed to a look of ghastly terror. They saw his face only for an instant before the window slammed shut and Jekyll was gone. That brief glimpse had been enough to chill them to the bone. Both men left the court in silence. It was not until they'd walked some way that Utterson turned to look at his cousin.

They were both pale and shaken.

'God forgive us, God forgive us,' said Mr Utterson.

CHAPTER 8

The Last Night

Mr Utterson was sitting by the fire one night after dinner, when he was surprised to receive a visit from Poole.

'Bless me, Poole, what brings you here?' he cried. Then seeing his face, he added, 'What's the matter, man? Is the doctor ill?'

'Mr Utterson,' the butler said, 'there is something wrong.'

The lawyer poured Poole a glass of wine and sat him down by the fire. 'Now take your time,' he said, 'and tell me why you've come.'

'You know the doctor's odd ways, sir,' replied Poole. 'How he shuts himself away. Well, he's shut himself in the office, and I don't like it, sir. On my life I don't like it, Mr Utterson, sir, I'm scared.'

'Now, my good man,' said the lawyer. 'Come to the point. What are you afraid of?'

Poole ignored the question. 'I've been afraid for about a week, sir, and I can't bear it no more.'

Everything about Poole's behaviour spoke of terror. Not once since his arrival had he looked the lawyer in the face. Even now his drink sat untasted on his knee and he stared at a corner of the carpet without raising his eyes. 'I can bear it no more,' he repeated.

'Come,' said Utterson. 'I see there's something wrong. Try to tell me what it is.'

'I think there's been some foul play,' the butler croaked hoarsely.

'Foul play!' cried the lawyer, now scared himself and losing all patience. 'What foul play do you mean? Spit it out, man!'

'I dare not say, sir. But will you come with me and see for yourself?' begged Poole.

Mr Utterson answered by rising to get his hat and coat. He noticed the great relief on Poole's face. The butler even left his wine on the table without tasting a drop.

◆◆◆

It was a wild, cold night as they set out for Jekyll's house. The wind made talking difficult and it almost seemed that it had swept every soul off the streets of the city. Mr Utterson had never seen that part of London look so deserted. He wished it was busier since he felt a strong desire for company. As they walked he couldn't shake off a strong sense that some fearful disaster lay in store for them.

When they reached Jekyll's house on the square,

Poole paused on the pavement and mopped the sweat from his brow with a red handkerchief. His face was white and his voice was harsh and broken.

'Well, sir,' he said, 'here we are, and I pray to God that nothing is wrong.'

'Amen to that, Poole,' said the lawyer.

The servant knocked on the door softly and it was opened on a chain.

'Is that you, Poole?' said the wary voice of a maid.

'It's all right,' said Poole. 'You can open the door.'

The hall was brightly lit and the fire was built up high. Around it every servant in the house stood huddled like a flock of sheep. At the sight of Utterson, the housemaid started whimpering and the cook cried out, 'Thank God! It's Mr Utterson!'

'What are you all doing here?' asked the lawyer with a frown. 'Your master would be most displeased.'

'They're all afraid,' said Poole. A long silence followed, broken only by the maid weeping loudly.

'Hold your tongue!' shouted Poole, betraying his own anxious state of mind. Utterson noticed every face kept turning towards the door to the laboratory with a look of dread.

'Now hand me a candle,' Poole said to one of the servant boys, 'and we'll get this over with quickly. Follow me, if you please, Mr Utterson.'

Poole led the way through the back garden. Before they entered the laboratory he whispered, 'Follow as quietly as you can, sir. I want you to hear but I don't want you to be heard. And see here, sir, if by any chance he asks you to go in, don't you go for any reason.'

Utterson's nerves were already on edge. This unexpected warning only threw him more off balance. Taking a deep breath, he followed Poole into the laboratory and through the litter of crates and bottles on the floor. At the foot of the stairs to Jekyll's office, Poole motioned to him to stop and listen. With a great effort of will, Poole climbed the stairs and knocked with a trembling hand on the door.

'Mr Utterson, sir, come to see you,' he called.

A voice answered from inside. 'Tell him I cannot see anyone,' it said.

'Thank you, sir,' said Poole. He looked at Utterson almost with triumph.

Utterson followed the butler back across the yard and into the great kitchen where the fire had died out.

Poole looked Utterson right in the eye. 'Now, sir, was that my master's voice?' he asked.

'It seems much changed,' replied the lawyer, shaking his head.

'Changed? I should say so,' said the butler. 'I've served my master for twenty years and if anyone knows his voice it's me. No, sir, my master's been done away with.'

'Done away with?' echoed Utterson in amazement. 'What do you mean, Poole?'

'I mean he was murdered eight days ago when we heard him cry out in the name of God. But who that thing is in there and why it stays there, is beyond all reason.'

'This is a wild tale, Poole,' said Utterson, shaking his head. 'Just say that it's true, say that Dr Jekyll has been . . . well murdered, why would the murderer stay in there? That doesn't hold water. It doesn't make any sense at all.'

'Well, you're a hard one to convince,' said Poole. 'But you haven't heard the full story yet. All this last week he or it, or whatever is in that room, has been crying day and night for some kind of medicine. It was sometimes the master's way to write his orders on a piece of paper and leave it on the stairs . . . '

'What kind of orders?' asked Utterson.

'For powders and medicines and such like,' said Poole. 'Well, all this week the door's been closed and we've had to leave food on the stairs to be smuggled in when nobody's around. Two or three times a day he's left orders and I've been sent running to every chemist in town. Yet every time I brought the stuff back, there'd be another message complaining and telling me to take it back because it wasn't pure. Then I'd get another order to a different chemist.'

'Whatever this medicine is, he obviously needs it badly,' said Utterson. 'Have you kept any of these papers?'

Poole felt in his pockets and brought out a crumpled piece of paper. Bending nearer to the candle, Utterson examined the writing.

The last sentence was scrawled wildly as if the writer had finally lost control of his feelings.

'This is a strange note,' said Utterson. 'How do you come to have opened it, Poole?'

To Maw's Chemists

Sir

The last sample is impure and quite useless for my purpose. Some years ago I purchased a large quantity from your shop. I now beg you to search for the original sample. If any of the same quality is left, please send it to me at once. Money is no object. I can hardly exaggerate the importance of this.

For God's sake find me some of the old!

Dr H Jekyll

'The man at Maw's was so angry he threw it back at me,' said the butler.

'And you're sure it's the doctor's handwriting?'

'It looks like it to me,' said Poole.

'Yet you said you feared your master was dead. How do you explain the notes?'

'I don't, sir. But what's that matter? I've seen him!'

'Seen him?' said the lawyer. 'When?'

'I came into the laboratory from the garden one evening. He must have slipped out from the office to look for whatever it is he's after. There he was at the far end of the room digging among the crates. He looked up when I came in, then gave a kind of cry and darted back

up the stairs.'

'And how did your master look?' said Utterson.

'My master?' said Poole. 'Sir, that thing was not my master. I only saw him for a minute but it made the hair stand up on the back of my neck. If that was my master why was he wearing a mask? And why did he cry out and run away from me?'

Poole passed a hand over his eyes as if to wipe the memory away.

'This is all very odd,' said Utterson. 'But I think I can see an explanation. Your master, Poole, has one of these rare illnesses that affect the patient's face. That is why he wore the mask and that's why he's been avoiding his friends. It's obvious the poor soul hopes to recover by finding the remedy he's seeking.'

'Sir,' replied the butler, 'that thing was not my master and that's the truth.' He dropped his voice to a whisper. 'My master is a tall well-built man, and this was a stunted fellow.'

Utterson opened his mouth to argue but Poole went on.

'Oh, sir! Do you think I don't know my own master after twenty years? No, sir, that thing in the mask was not Dr Jekyll. God knows what it was, but it wasn't him. It's my belief my master's been murdered.'

'Poole, if you keep saying that, then it's my duty to

find out,' said Utterson. 'Much as I want to spare your master's feelings I shall be forced to break down that door.'

'Now you're talking, sir!' cried the butler.

'And who'll help me do it?' said Utterson.

Poole hesitated a moment, struggling to overcome his terror. Then he spoke with grim determination.

'I will, sir. There is an axe in the laboratory and you can take the kitchen poker.'

CHAPTER 9

The Secret Behind the Door

Taking the heavy poker, Utterson weighed it in his hand and looked at his companion.

'You realize, Poole,' he said, 'that you and I are about to place ourselves in some danger?'

'You may say so, sir,' said the servant.

'It's time we spoke freely then,' said Utterson. 'That figure in the mask, did you recognize him?'

'Well, sir,' said Poole. 'It was only an instant and he was bent over double. But if you mean was it Mr Hyde? Why yes, I think it was! You see it was about his size and had that same light way of moving. And then who else could have got in the laboratory door? Remember after the murder he still had the key with him?'

Utterson nodded in reply.

'But that's not all,' said Poole. 'Have you ever met this Hyde, sir?'

'Yes,' said the lawyer. 'I spoke to him once.'

'Then you'll remember there was an odd feeling about him. Something that gave a man a strange turn. I don't know how else to describe it but you felt a kind of creeping in your flesh.'

'I know what you mean,' said Utterson. 'I've felt it too.'

'Well,' Poole continued. 'When that masked monkey jumped out from the crates and whipped into the office, I felt that same chill run down my spine like ice. Oh, I know it's not evidence for a judge and jury, but I know what I felt. I'd swear on my life that was Mr Hyde!'

'My thoughts have been running the same way,' said Utterson. 'I always feared no good would come of your master knowing Hyde. Now I fear that poor Jekyll has been murdered and his killer is still lurking in that room – though God alone knows why. Well it's time he was brought to justice. Call Bradshaw.'

The footman arrived looking pale and nervous.

'Pull yourself together, Bradshaw,' said the lawyer. 'This waiting has set you all on edge, but now we are going to bring it to an end. Poole and I are going to break down the door of the office. If there's nothing the matter inside, then I will take the blame. But if we're right, there may be a wanted criminal in there. You and the boy must stop him escaping by the back. Be ready at the laboratory door with two good strong sticks. We'll give you ten minutes to get to your stations.'

The lawyer checked his watch and led the way into the yard, gripping the poker in one hand. Clouds had passed over the moon and the sky was inky black. The wind blew the candle's flame back and forth making their shadows leap and dance on the wall. They sat down to wait outside the laboratory. The hum of the city seemed far way. Close at hand they could clearly hear footsteps walking to and fro in the office.

'It walks like that all day,' whispered Poole. 'Sometimes half the night too. There's only a pause when a new sample comes from the chemist. Ah it's a bad conscience that cannot sleep. But listen carefully, sir and tell me – is that the doctor's footsteps?'

Utterson listened. The steps fell lightly and oddly, nothing like the heavy tread of Henry Jekyll. Utterson sighed. 'Is there never any other sound?'

Poole nodded. 'Once. Once I heard it weeping.'

'Weeping? How?' asked Utterson.

'Like a woman or some lost soul,' said the butler. 'The

sound was so mournful that I could have wept myself.'

The ten minutes for Bradshaw to be ready had passed. Poole fetched the axe from under a pile of packing straw. They left the candle on a table to light their way to the office door. Hardly daring to breathe, they drew nearer to where the footsteps still paced up and down, up and down.

'Jekyll!' cried Utterson in a loud voice. 'I demand to

see you.' He paused for a moment but no reply came. 'I give you fair warning,' he went on, 'our suspicions are aroused and I must see you. If you don't open the door we'll break it down by force.'

'Utterson,' said the voice, 'for God's sake have mercy!'

'Ah, that's not Jekyll's voice – it's Hyde's!' cried Utterson. 'Break down the door, Poole!'

Poole swung the axe and the blow shook the whole building. A screech of animal terror rang out from behind the door. The axe swung again and the panels splintered. Four times the blow fell but the wood was strong and the hinges were well made. It wasn't until the fifth blow that the lock broke and the wreckage of the door fell inwards on the carpet.

Poole and Utterson peered in though the doorway. After the deafening noise of their siege, all was silent. The room at first sight seemed ordered and peaceful. The fire burned in the hearth, the kettle sang softly above it and a cup and saucer was laid out for tea. Leaving aside the bottles of chemicals, it could have been the most ordinary room in London.

In the middle of the floor lay the body of a man still twitching. They went over to it and turned it over on its back. The face that they looked on was Edward Hyde's. He was dressed in clothes far too big for him, clothes that would have fitted the doctor. The muscles in his face

were still moving, but the breath had gone from his body. His hand gripped a small glass bottle from which came a strong smell. Utterson guessed it was some kind of poison. They were looking on the body of a man who had just killed himself.

'We're too late to save or punish him,' said the lawyer. 'Hyde is gone to his Maker. All we can do is to look for the body of Dr Jekyll.'

◆◆◆

They searched the laboratory and the office from top to bottom. Down some steps they found a large cellar filled with nothing but cobwebs. They could find no trace of Henry Jekyll dead or alive.

Poole stamped on the stone floor and listened. 'He must be buried here somewhere,' he said.

'Either that or he escaped,' said Utterson. He examined the door that Hyde had used as his secret entrance from the back street. The door was locked and on the ground they found the key, already brown with rust.

'This doesn't look like it's been used,' said the lawyer.

'Used, sir?' said Poole. 'Can't you see it's broken? As if someone had stamped on it.'

The two men looked at each other. 'This is a mystery,' said Utterson.

They returned to the office in silence and began a more careful search. On a table they found a white powder, like salt, measured onto glass saucers as if for some unfinished experiment.

'That is the same stuff that I was always bringing him,' said Poole.

The tea things stood ready by an armchair with sugar in the cup. Next to them a book of religion lay open. Foul comments in Jekyll's handwriting were scrawled in the margins. A large full length mirror stood in its frame, turned upwards towards the ceiling.

'This mirror has seen some strange things,' whispered Poole.

'Yes,' agreed the lawyer. 'But why keep a full-size mirror in an office?'

Next they searched the desk. Among a neat pile of papers, they found a large envelope with the name of Utterson written in Jekyll's handwriting.

Utterson opened it and several pieces of paper fell to the floor. The first was a will drawn up in the same odd terms as the one Utterson had given back to Jekyll six months before. Yet in place of the name of Edward Hyde, the lawyer was amazed to see his own name – Gabriel John Utterson. He looked at Poole and then at the body of the murderer lying on the floor.

'I don't understand,' he said. 'The will has been here

with Hyde for days. It must have driven him wild to see himself replaced by me. So why didn't he destroy it?'

He picked up the next piece of paper that was written in the doctor's handwriting and dated at the top.

'Poole!' said Utterson. 'He was alive and here today! His body can't have been disposed of with such little time. He must still be alive, he must have escaped!'

'Why don't you read the note, sir?' asked Poole.

'Because I'm afraid to,' replied the lawyer gravely. With an effort he looked down at the paper and started to read.

My dear Utterson

By the time you read this I shall have disappeared, how I don't know, but the end is surely near and must come soon. Go then and first read the letter that Lanyon left behind for you. If you want to know more, turn to the full confession of

Your unworthy and unhappy friend

Henry Jekyll

'Was there a third envelope?' asked Utterson.

Poole handed him a large packet, sealed in several

places. The lawyer put it in his pocket. 'Say nothing about this to anyone,' he warned Poole. 'It's now ten o'clock. I must go home and read these papers, but I'll be back before midnight and then we'll send for the police.'

They left the laboratory and Utterson set off back to his office to read the two letters that would explain the whole mystery.

CHAPTER 10

Dr Lanyon's Story

Utterson reached into his safe and took out Lanyon's letter, the one that he'd received just before Lanyon had died. On the envelope it said, *'Not to be opened until the death or disappearance of Dr Henry Jekyll.'* That time had come. Utterson ripped open the envelope and read what Lanyon had written inside.

On the 9th January, I received a letter from my old school friend Henry Jekyll. I was surprised at this. I had been to Jekyll's house for a supper party the night before, but we weren't in the habit of writing to each other. Why hadn't Jekyll spoken to me when he had the chance? When I began to read my wonder only increased. This is what the letter said:

Dear Lanyon

You are one of my oldest friends. We may have differed on questions of science, but you have always been dear to me. If at any time you had said to me, 'Jekyll, my life, my honour, and my reason depend on you,' I would have gone to any length to help you. Lanyon, my life, my honour, and my reason are all at your mercy. If you don't help me tonight I am lost.

I want you to put off all other business for tonight, and take a cab with this letter in your hand to my house. Poole, my butler, has orders from me and you'll find him waiting for you. A locksmith will also be there. The door to my office must be forced open and you are to enter alone. Go to my desk and open the fourth drawer from the top (or the third from the bottom which is the same thing.) In my present state of mind, I dread giving you wrong instructions, but you'll know the right drawer by what's inside. You'll find some powders, a small bottle, and a notebook. Take the drawer and carry it back to your house, just as it is.

That's the first part of my request, now for the second. You should be back long before midnight, when the servants will be in bed. At midnight I want you to wait alone in your consulting room. A man will come to your door and mention my name. I want you to give him the drawer. Then you will have played your part and earned my heartfelt gratitude.

These requests may sound strange, perhaps even mad, but if you disobey any one of them, I swear that it may cause my death.

Think of me at this hour, in a strange place and filled with a blackness I cannot describe. Yet if you will only help me, I know my troubles will roll away like a story that is told. My dear Lanyon, please help me and save me.

Your friend

Henry Jekyll

PS If the post office doesn't deliver this letter to you today it may already be too late. In that case do what I ask and expect my messenger at midnight tomorrow. If no one comes, you'll know that you've seen the last of me.'

When I'd finished reading this letter, I was convinced that Henry Jekyll had lost his mind. Nevertheless, while there was any doubt, I felt bound to obey his requests.

A letter of this kind couldn't be ignored. I rose straight away and took a cab to Jekyll's house.

Poole was waiting for me with a locksmith and a carpenter. Together we went through the laboratory to Jekyll's office. The door was strong and the lock was well made but between the locksmith and the carpenter we eventually had it open. I took out the drawer that Jekyll had described and had it filled up with straw and tied in a sheet. With the contents safe from spilling I carried it back to my house.

Once home I started to examine what was in the drawer. The powders were white crystals rather like salt and obviously made up by Jekyll himself. The bottle was half full of a blood-red liquid which had a strong smell. The other ingredients were unfamiliar to me. When I looked in the notebook it seemed to contain nothing but a series of dates covering a period of several years. The entries came to an end abruptly at a date nearly a year ago. Here and there were brief comments next to a date. 'Double,' was one and early in the list were the words 'Total failure!!!'

All this told me very little. Jekyll had obviously been using the chemicals for some experiment that had led to

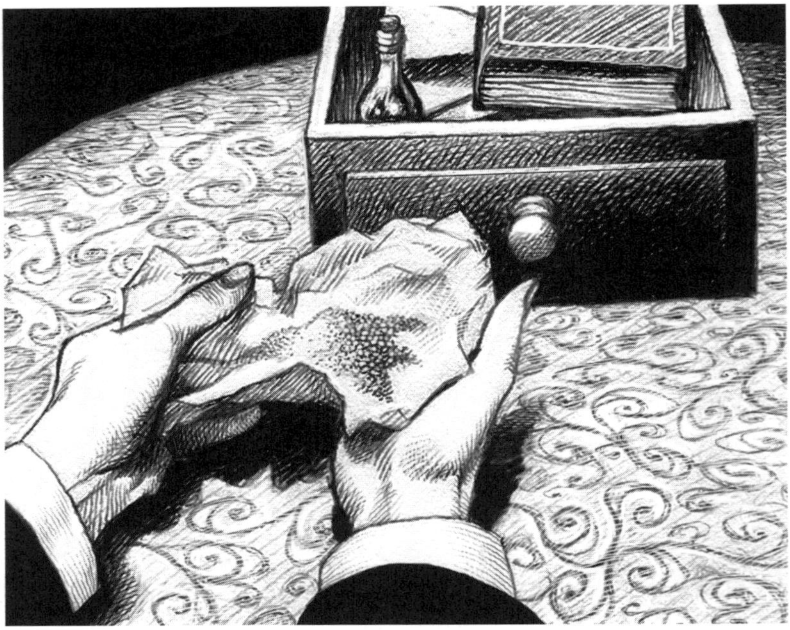

no earthly use (like most of his investigations). How could the contents of the drawer possibly save his life? If his messenger could come to my house why couldn't he go to Jekyll's office? And why all the secrecy?

The more I pondered these questions the more I felt I was dealing with a madman. After sending my servants to bed I loaded a revolver and sat waiting for midnight.

The clock had hardly struck twelve when there was a soft knock on my door. Opening up I found a small man crouched in the porch.

'Have you come from Dr Jekyll?' I asked.

He answered with a nod, glancing behind him all the time. There was a policeman walking the square and my visitor seemed anxious to come inside out of his sight.

His behaviour made me uneasy and I kept my hand on the revolver as I followed him into my consulting room.

In the light I could see him clearly. He was small, with an unhealthy appearance. I was also aware of a strong reaction in myself caused by his company. At the time I thought it was just a personal dislike, but I've since thought it was something deeper than that. His clothes would have made an ordinary person look comical. They were enormously too large for him. The trousers were rolled up to stop them getting under his feet and the waist of the coat almost came down to his thighs. There was something unnatural about him, something strange and revolting.

These judgements I made in a few seconds, my visitor was on fire with eagerness.

'Have you got it? Have you got it?' he cried, laying his hand on my arm.

I shook him off, feeling an icy chill at his touch.

'Come, sir,' I said. 'You forget that I haven't had the pleasure of meeting you. Please be seated.'

'I beg your pardon, Dr Lanyon,' he replied politely enough. 'I was forgetting my manners. I've come from Henry Jekyll on important business. And I understood . . . '

He paused and clutched at his throat. 'I understood, a drawer . . .'

I took pity on him and pointed to the drawer, covered over with the sheet. 'There it is, sir,' I said.

He leapt over to it and then paused. I could hear his teeth grating together and his face was so white and ghastly that I began to fear for my own safety.

'Pull yourself together, sir,' I said. He turned a dreadful smile on me and threw off the sheet. At the sight of what was in the drawer he gave a loud sob of relief. The next moment he had himself under control and asked, 'Have you a measuring glass?'

I gave him what he asked. He began to mix up some kind of chemical potion with the powders and the liquid. At first it was reddish in colour, then it began to bubble and give off clouds of steam. Finally, the bubbling ceased and the mixture darkened to purple and then, more slowly, to a watery green. My visitor had watched all this with satisfaction. Now he smiled, set the glass down on the table and turned to me.

'And now it's for you to decide. If you take my advice, you'll let me take this glass and leave your house without any delay or explanation. Or is your curiosity too strong to permit that? Think carefully before you answer, the choice is yours. If you command me to stay I can promise you a sight which would stagger the devil himself.'

I spoke calmly though I was far from feeling from it. 'Sir, you speak in riddles and you won't be surprised if I don't believe you. But I've had enough of riddles for one night. I've gone too far to stop before I'm given an explanation.'

'Very well,' replied my visitor. 'Remember your vows as a doctor, what you see is between you and I. And now, Lanyon, you who have always held to the narrowest views, you have scoffed at your superiors – behold and learn!'

He put the glass to his lips and drank it at one gulp. A second later, he cried out, staggered, and clutched at the table. As he stared and gasped, I thought I saw a change

in him. He seemed to swell up. His face turned suddenly dark and the features began to melt and alter. The next moment I had sprung to my feet and backed against the wall, my arm raised to shield me from that terrifying sight.

'Oh God!' I cried out. 'Oh God!'

There before my eyes – pale, shaken, like a man back from the dead – stood Henry Jekyll!

What he told me in the next hour, I cannot bring myself to write. I only know I saw what I saw and heard what I heard and it sickened me to my soul. My life has been shaken to the roots. I cannot sleep and I feel a deadly terror day and night. I feel that my days are numbered and I will die. And yet I will die unable to believe what I've seen.

As for what Jekyll told me with tears of regret, I cannot think of it without horror. I will say only one thing, Utterson. The creature who crept into my house that night, is known by the name of Edward Hyde. He is hunted in every corner of the land as the murderer of Sir Danvers Carew.

Hastie Lanyon

CHAPTER II

Henry Jekyll's Full Confession

I was born into a good family and with a large fortune. I'm the first to admit that I was given every chance of a successful future. My worst fault was a taste for low pleasures and amusement. I found this hard to combine with my desire to appear serious in public. So it came about that I began to keep my pleasures secret and led a double life. Not that I did anything very shameful, but in time I began to think of myself as not one but two people. Both sides of me were equal parts of my nature – the scientist and the pleasure seeker, the public Jekyll and the one who roamed the city after dark.

Slowly, I began to believe that man is not one personality, but two (or even more). I started to dream of separating these two sides of myself. Wouldn't life be much more enjoyable, I asked myself, if we didn't have to struggle with the good and bad sides of our character? Why shouldn't the good and bad personalities each be free to go their own way?

At this point my scientific studies shed some light on the question. I began to see that the flesh of our body is much less solid than we think. I will not bore you with

the science of my investigations. It's enough to say that I managed to make a potion. This potion allowed me to cast off my normal body and replace it with a new one – a body for the evil side of my character.

I hesitated for a long time before putting my idea to the test. I knew that I was risking death with the experiment. By the least mistake or overdose I could destroy the body which I was trying to change. But the temptation to discover something so incredible, soon overcame my fears. I bought a large quantity of a powder from a chemists which provided the last ingredient I required for my experiment. Late one dark night, I mixed up the potion, watched it bubble and smoke in the glass, and drank it down to the last drop.

I was immediately in the grip of the most terrible pains. I felt sick, my bones seemed to grind together, and I felt a terror in my soul like the fear of death. When these pains started to ease, I came to myself like a man recovering from a heavy sickness. I was aware of something strange and new. I felt younger, lighter, happier in my body. At the same time I was aware of a new freedom and boldness. I felt my new self to be ten times as wicked as the old Jekyll. I was purely evil and the thought delighted me. I stretched out my hands to feel my new body and instantly realized that I was smaller.

At that time I didn't have a mirror in my room. (I bought one later to watch myself changing.)

It was the early hours of the morning and the first

light of dawn was not far off. Excited by my success, I decided to go as far as my bedroom. I crossed the yard under the stars and crept through the corridors of the house. Coming to my room, I went straight to the mirror. There I saw for the first time the appearance of Edward Hyde.

I can only guess that the evil side of my nature was less healthy and developed than my good side. (After all, I'd spent most of my life trying to be good.) It followed that Edward Hyde was smaller, thinner, and younger than Henry Jekyll. Just as Jekyll had a kind, good face, evil was written plainly on the face of Hyde. Evil had also given him a body that looked ugly and unhealthy. Yet when I looked at my other self in the mirror, I didn't feel any hatred. This self was part of me. It seemed natural and human. In my eyes, Hyde was more full of life and spirit than Jekyll. I have since noticed that when I am Edward Hyde no one can come near me without a visible shrinking back. This, I imagine, is because most people are a mixture of good and evil – only Hyde is pure evil.

I didn't stay long at my bedroom mirror. Only one part of my experiment was complete. I still had to find out whether I could return myself to the body of Henry Jekyll. The thought that I might fail – and remain imprisoned as Hyde for ever – was one I dared not contemplate. Once more I prepared the cup and drank it, once more I suffered the pains of my body changing. When I came to myself I had the face and character of Henry Jekyll again.

That night I came to a fatal crossroads. At that time evil was a stronger force in me than good. Evil seized its chance and Edward Hyde stepped forward. Henry Jekyll was still a confused mix of good and bad, Hyde on the other hand was pure evil. The worse side of me had the upper hand.

I could have stopped there, but the temptation to go on was too strong. I was by now a highly-respected doctor but I found the life of study dry and dull. Hyde offered me the perfect escape. I had only to drink the cup and I could shrug off the body of the noted professor and step into the body of Edward Hyde. I smiled at the idea, it almost seemed like a good joke. I began to make preparations for my strange new life. I rented a house in Soho and employed a housekeeper to keep the place. Next I drew up that will, Utterson, which you disliked so much. If anything happened to me as Dr Jekyll, I knew I could continue as Edward Hyde and still enjoy my fortune.

When all this was done I felt I was ready to enjoy

my double life.

Other men have hired villains to do their crimes for them. I was the first to be able to do anything I liked. In public I was respectable, but in a moment I could throw off my other life and escape to freedom. And whatever I did as Hyde I was safe. Just think – I did not even exist! All I had to do was return to my laboratory and drink the potion and Edward Hyde would vanish like the mist. In his place would be Henry Jekyll – a man who could sit quietly at home in all innocence.

The pleasures I'd known in my old life had been foolish. As Hyde, the things I began to do were monstrous. When I returned from one of my late night adventures, I often wondered at the evil things I'd done. Hyde was a creature of foul wickedness. Everything he did was done for himself and he cared nothing for the pain he caused anyone else. At times Henry Jekyll watched appalled at the things that Edward Hyde did. But it was Hyde and Hyde alone who was guilty. Jekyll could wake again to his good self and even try to put right the things that Hyde had done wrong. In this way my conscience didn't trouble me.

I have no wish to go into detail about the things that I did as Hyde. I only want to trace the steps that led to my ultimate fall and punishment. One accident led to a moment of danger. I knocked down a child in the street and a passer-by saw what happened. (The witness, I recognized the other day as your cousin, Mr Enfield.) The doctor and the child's family joined in the threats against me. In order to appease them Edward Hyde had to bring them to the door and pay them a cheque made out in the name of Henry Jekyll. To avoid such a danger in the future I opened a bank account in the name of Edward Hyde. I even supplied my double with a signature by sloping my handwriting backwards. I imagined that I was safe from any fear of discovery.

Two months before the night of Carew's murder, my world was shaken. I had returned late at night from one my adventures as Hyde. As usual I had drunk the potion and returned to the body of Henry Jekyll. When I woke the next day I felt that something was wrong. The room looked the same and the pattern on my bed curtains was just as it always was. Yet something inside me kept insisting I was not in the right place. I looked down at my hand. Henry Jekyll's hand was large, white, and firm, but the hand I was staring at was small and covered with rough hair. It was the hand of Edward Hyde!

For half a minute I stared stupidly at my own hand. Then I awoke to a feeling of terror and jumped out of bed. Rushing to the mirror I looked at my reflection. At

the sight of myself my blood turned to ice. I had gone to bed as Henry Jekyll and woken up as Edward Hyde. How could it have happened? More to the point, how was I to save myself? By now the servants were up and moving around, but all my medicines were in my office. It was a long journey to make downstairs and across the yard without being seen. Even if I covered my face, how was I to hide my shrunken body? Then, with great relief, I remembered that the servants were used to Hyde coming and going. I dressed quickly in clothes that were far too big and went downstairs. Poole passed me in the hall and stared at my clothes in surprise. Ten minutes later Dr Jekyll had returned to his own shape and was sitting down to breakfast.

I had little appetite. It seemed to me that I had received a terrible warning. I thought back trying to explain what had happened. Lately it had seemed to me that Edward Hyde had grown stronger and even bigger. I began to glimpse the danger that, if things went on, the power to change myself back would be lost. I would be stuck for all time as Edward Hyde. The power of the potion to change me hadn't always been the same. Once, early on in my experiments, it had failed me completely. Since then I'd had to double and even treble the amount that I drank. Now I was forced to admit that a change had taken place without my noticing. Where it had once been hard to throw off the body of Jekyll, now it was Hyde who clung to me. Everything pointed to the truth that I was losing hold of my better self and the evil character of Hyde was tightening its grip on me.

I knew that I'd come to a point where I had to choose. My two selves remembered each other but had little else in common. Jekyll was greedy for the pleasures and adventures of Hyde. Hyde, on the other hand, cared nothing for Jekyll. He only remembered him as the dark cave he ran to when he was in trouble. Jekyll had a father's affection for Hyde, Hyde was as indifferent as the most ungrateful son. I knew that if I chose

Jekyll I'd lose all those dark secret pleasures I'd started to enjoy. Yet if I chose Hyde all my ambitions would die at one stroke. I'd become despised and friendless. The choice may seem an obvious one but it's the old struggle between good and evil. What I did was much the same as many others before me. I chose the right path but I didn't have the strength to keep to it.

Yes, I chose Jekyll – the ageing doctor with his friends and his honest hopes. I said goodbye to the youth, freedom, and the secret adventures of Hyde. Perhaps some part of me held back because I didn't burn Hyde's clothes or give up the house in Soho. For two months I was true to my promise and led a blameless life. But in time I forgot the force of the warning I'd received. I began to be tortured with longing as if Hyde was struggling to get free inside me. At last, in an hour of weakness, I made up the potion again and drank it down.

I hadn't bargained for the depths of Hyde's evil, but this is how I was punished. It was as if Hyde was a caged lion and he came out roaring. Even as I changed my shape I was aware of a furious evil energy. When I walked out after dark that night, as Hyde, I was looking for someone to vent my rage on. Danvers Carew was the unlucky victim. Only a madman could have attacked a stranger like that without any reason. But I – or Hyde I should say – was like a sick child breaking a toy. Something within me delighted in every blow I struck.

When it was done the mist of rage cleared from my eyes. I saw what I'd done and felt a cold thrill of terror. I was a murderer. I would be hunted down and hung at the gallows.

I ran to my house in Soho and burned all my papers in the fire. When I set off home to Jekyll's house I still felt light-headed. Even as I mixed up the potion I smiled and drank a toast to the dead man. A few seconds later Hyde was replaced by Henry Jekyll who broke down in tears. As Jekyll, I went down on my knees and asked God's forgiveness for what I'd done. Through my tears I saw myself clearly. I saw my whole life, from the days of my childhood to this night of horror. I tried with prayers to smother the horrible pictures that my memory brought to the surface. I could have screamed out loud.

One thing was certain – from this day my choice was made. To become Edward Hyde was now impossible, whether I wanted him or not. Hyde was a murderer, a wanted man. I was now stuck with my better self and how glad I felt! I locked the door that Hyde had used to come and go and ground the key under my heel.

The next day I heard the news that there had been a witness to the murder. Hyde's guilt was known to the world and the man he'd murdered was a person of high

standing. It had been more than a crime, it had been an act of sheer madness. I think I was almost glad of this news. My vow never to let Hyde loose in the world again was strengthened by the terror of the hangman's noose. Jekyll was now my safe harbour, if Hyde was to peep out for just a second, the law would hunt him down as a killer.

I promised myself I would make amends for the past and I can say with honesty that some good came out of my promise. You'll remember the two months at the end of last year, Utterson? How I worked to help others and relieve their suffering? You'll remember the dinner parties held at my house? As the quiet days went by I began to be grateful for my old life and its routine pleasures. Yet the two sides of my personality still existed and as my shame wore off, so the lower side of me began to growl for attention like a chained dog. Not that I ever dreamed of taking the shape of Hyde again. The mere thought was enough to bring me back to my senses. Yet I was tempted and I was too weak to resist.

I remember the day clearly. It was a bright January day, the frost had melted and Regent's Park was full of the birds singing and the sweet smell of spring. I was sitting in the sun on a bench and feeling quite content with myself. After all, I thought, I was much like anyone else. In fact I was better than some, at least I did some good in the world, where other people I could name followed their own selfish pleasures. At this very moment of pride, a strange feeling came over me. It was like a shudder, a horrible wave of sickness. The feeling soon passed and left me rather faint. Then the faintness was replaced by a different sensation. I felt bolder, free to do what I wanted and careless of danger. When I looked down I noticed that my clothes hung loosely on my shrunken body. My hand on my knee was hairy and knuckled. Once again, without any warning, I had changed into Edward Hyde. A moment before I had been safe, wealthy, and comfortable – now I was hunted and homeless, a wanted murderer.

You can imagine my fear and confusion. Yet I was still able to think clearly. I have noticed that when in my evil shape my senses seem to be sharper and more cunning. Where Jekyll would have been all at sea, Hyde rose to the challenge of the moment.

I sat with my head in my hands trying to work out a way to save myself. My problem was this: the ingredients for the potion were in a drawer in my office, how was I to get them?

I had locked the back door to the laboratory myself. If I tried to enter through my own house I would be seen by my servants and they would call the police. The only answer was for someone else to go to my office for me. Immediately I thought of Lanyon. But how was I to contact him and persuade him to what I asked? Even if I could visit the doctor – why would he listen to a man like Hyde and break into his friend's office? Then the answer came to me. One part of my old self still remained – my handwriting. Once I had thought of sending Lanyon a letter, the rest of the plan fell into place.

I called for a cab and ordered the driver to take me to a hotel in Portland Street. The driver took one look at my baggy clothes and couldn't help laughing. I flew into a rage and the smile was soon wiped from his face. (Lucky for him or I would have dragged him out of his seat.) At the hotel, I gave the staff such black looks that they quickly gave me a room and didn't ask any questions. I ordered the porter to bring me pen and paper so that I could write a letter. Hyde, with his life in danger, was revealing a new side of his character. He was shaking with anger and longing to make somebody suffer. Yet the creature was cunning. He mastered his rage and wrote his two important letters, one to Lanyon and one to Poole.

After that he sat all day in his private room, biting his

nails. He ate alone with his fears and waited for the night to come. When darkness fell he called a cab and drove around the streets of the city until the hour of his appointment with Lanyon. You'll notice I say he, not I. That child of hell was not me. There was nothing human in him, nothing but fear and hatred. When at last the cab driver began to grow suspicious Hyde got out and began to walk the streets of the city. He walked fast, hunted by his fears and chattering to himself all the time. He kept to dark back alleys away from people and counted the minutes until midnight. Once a woman spoke to him, offering a box of matches. He lashed out at her and she ran away.

When I reached Dr Lanyon's I was startled by the look of horror on his face. It was nothing in comparison to the loathing I felt for the hours that I'd passed that evening. A change had come over me. It wasn't just the fear of the gallows that gnawed at me, it was the dread of being Hyde. I spoke to Lanyon and made up the potion in a dream. Still in a dream, I came home to my house and got into bed. I slept so deeply that not even nightmares could break my slumbers. In the morning I woke up, weak but refreshed. I still hated and feared the thought of Hyde, but I felt safe back in my own home and near to my powders and medicines. I was so grateful for my escape that I almost felt hopeful.

After breakfast, I went out in the yard to breathe some fresh air and feel the cool wind on my face. Suddenly I clutched at the wall. The shuddering and the waves of sickness were coming over me again. I only had a few seconds to run to my office before I was again raging and cursing in the hated shape of Hyde.

This time it took a double dose of the potion to restore me to my old self. To my horror it didn't last. Only six hours later, as I sat staring into the fire, the pangs returned. I had to mix and drink the potion once again. From that day on it seemed that it was only with a great effort and repeated doses of the potion, that I could hold onto the body of Henry Jekyll. At any hour of the day and night I would start to shudder and the change would begin again. If I dozed off or slept in my chair I always woke up to find I was Hyde again.

I was like a creature in a waking nightmare. I could not allow myself to sleep and paced the room to keep my eyes from closing. My body and mind were eaten up by fever. Only one thing drove me and that was the horror of my other self. When I slept or when the potion wore off, I would become Hyde. And now the change had started to happen almost without me noticing. When I was Hyde my body didn't seem strong enough to hold the raging energy of that demon. As Jekyll grew weaker by the day, Hyde seemed to grow stronger and stronger. The hatred they felt was equal on both sides now. Jekyll looked on Hyde as something hellish, a thing that was hardly human. Once he had taken pleasure in his lower self. Now he found it shocking. That creature of horror was joined to him closer than a wife. It lay caged in his body, muttering and struggling to get out and be born.

The hatred Hyde felt for Jekyll was of a different kind. His fear of the hangman's rope drove him to commit temporary suicide and become Jekyll. Yet he hated doing it. He despised Jekyll for giving up so easily and resented the way he was disliked. In revenge Hyde started to play ape-like tricks on me. He scrawled on the pages of my books, burnt my letters and even destroyed a painting of my father. If it wasn't for his fear of death, I'm sure he would have destroyed himself long ago, in order to destroy me too.

But his love of life is wonderful. Even though I sicken at the thought of him, I almost pity him. How he fears my power to put an end to him by suicide!

And now time is running out. It is useless for me to try and continue my story. No man has ever suffered such torments – let that be enough. My punishment might have gone on for years if it wasn't for the final disaster that has cut me off for ever from my own nature. My stock of the salty powder – essential to the potion – began to run low. (I have never needed to order more since the date of the first experiment.) I sent out for a fresh supply and used it to mix the drink. The bubbling followed as usual, then the change of colour to purple, but not the change to green. I drank the liquid down but it had no effect. You will know from Poole how I have sent to every chemist in London to try and find what I need. I have failed. I am now convinced that the first batch of my supply was impure. It was that unknown impurity that made it effective.

About a week has passed since I last wrote. I am now finishing this statement under the influence of the last of the old powders. This is the last time that Henry Jekyll can think his own thoughts and look on his own face in the mirror. I must bring my story to an end. These papers have only survived so far by a mixture of carefulness and good luck. If the change should happen while I'm still writing, Hyde will tear this paper to shreds. If I have time to put it away, I may save it from his vicious spite.

Already our doom is closing in on us both. Half an

hour from now I shall take on the hated character of Hyde for ever. I know I shall sit shuddering and weeping in my chair. I will pace up and down this room – my last refuge – dreading the sound of a footstep outside the door. Will Hyde die at the gallows? Or will he find the courage to put an end to his miserable life at the last minute? Only God knows, I cannot care any longer. This is my own hour of death and what follows is Hyde's fate not mine. Now as I lay down my pen and seal the envelope, I bring the unhappy life of Henry Jekyll to an end.